AF409731

Ecosystems

An Intricate Web of Life

ACKNOWLEDGEMENTS

This book would not have been possible without the support and inspiration of many individuals. First of all I extend my deepest gratitude to my Principal Prof.G.K.Jha and the ARSD College governing body for granting me a sabbatical to pursue my passion of studying in depth various ecosystems of the world. I am profoundly thankful to my husband G.R.Narang, son Utkarsh Narang, and daughter Unnati Narang without whose help I would have never been able to visit such diverse places of the globe and achieve my dream. I appreciate the support of my daughter in law Kamia Narang and son in law Joshua Camins. Above all, I am grateful to the Almighty for the blessings and guiding me at every step. This book is a testament to the beauty and complexity of the ecosystems God has created and I am honoured to share my knowledge with inputs from the available information to the world.

Dedicated to my parents

and

Love of my grandchildren

PREFACE

Our planet, the earth, is inhabited by a variety of organisms. These organisms interact not only with each other but also with their physical environment. Ecosystems are intricate networks of all living organisms present in an area interacting with their physical environment. The interconnectedness of ecosystems forms the intricate web of life where each component relies on others for survival. Understanding ecosystems is crucial for many reasons. They provide us with essential services, such as food, air, water, habitat, climate regulation, soil fertility, and many supporting and recreational services such as tourism, fishing, and forestry. These services are important for the well-being and survival of mankind. Any disturbance in the natural balance between the two components of the ecosystem i.e. the living and the physical factors affects the existence of surroundings as well as the organisms inhabiting the ecosystem. The book explores the diverse ecosystems across the globe, highlighting their unique characteristics, climate pattern, and interactions for sustainability. The focus is on the major ecosystems, both terrestrial and aquatic. A brief description of ecosystems of Asia (India, Bhutan, and Bali,

Indonesia), North America (USA and Canada), and Australia have been dealt with inputs from personal visits to some of the unique ecosystems in these parts of the globe. Through this exploration, I aim to foster a deeper understanding of the natural world and the importance of conserving its ecosystems by maintaining an ecological balance.

Ecosystems and their functioning

Ecosystem is an ecological unit that encompasses all forms of life occupying an area and their interactions with the physical environment, the soil, water, air etc.

Ernst Haeckel, a German zoologist in 1866 gave the term **Ecology** from the Greek word 'Oikos' that means home. He gave this word in context of fauna or the animals. However, by the year 1875 the word was translated into English and its meaning was broadened to include both plants and animals. Sir Arthur G. Tansley in 1935 gave the term Ecosystem. A living organism in an ecosystem depends on physical factors for continued survival.

The structure of the ecosystem comprises two components, abiotic and the biotic. Both these components are inseparable and interact with each other forming an ecosystem.

- The **Abiotic** component consists of physical factors like light, temperature, precipitation, atmospheric humidity, wind, and the soil.

- The **Biotic** component consists of the various living organisms that are the plants, animals and the microbes.

Plants are the producers that can trap the radiant energy of the sun and convert it into chemical energy through the process of photosynthesis. They can synthesize or produce food in the form of glucose in the presence of sunlight and the green pigment chlorophyll, present mainly in leaves of the plants. As plants can manufacture their own food they are referred to as autotrophs. The consumers that are the heterotrophs depend on producers or the autotrophs for their survival. The first level of consumers that feed on plants are called **primary consumers** followed by **secondary consumers** that feed on primary consumers followed by **tertiary consumers**, or the top-level consumers, that feed on primary and secondary consumers.

The interaction between the two components of the ecosystem creates a dynamic, self-sustaining functional unit that sustains life on the planet earth maintaining a stable environment and a natural balance.

The two main functions of the ecosystem are the **energy flow** and **nutrient cycling**.

The first function **Energy Flow** in an ecosystem can be explained by the laws of thermodynamics. The flow of energy follows the first law of thermodynamics according to which energy can neither be created nor destroyed. In the context of ecosystem study it is the radiant energy of the sun. Plants in the presence of this energy, fix atmospheric carbon dioxide to produce organic molecules during photosynthesis and release oxygen. Part of the energy is converted into chemical energy in the form of food and is used by heterotrophs, the consumers that cannot prepare their own food. When the plant eaters the primary consumers or the herbivores eat plants, they convert it into chemical energy and degrade part of the energy releasing heat. Further the degradation will occur at the level of secondary consumers and again at the level of tertiary consumers that are the top-level carnivores. The process of eating and being eaten is called the **Food Chain**. At each level of the food chain called the **trophic level**, energy is transferred in the form of food from the producers to primary consumers to secondary and to tertiary consumers. Producers represent the first trophic level, herbivores (primary consumers) the second trophic level and carnivores (secondary consumers) the third trophic level. The top carnivores (tertiary consumers) represent the last level of the food chain. Food chains do not operate in isolation in any ecosystem. At more than one trophic level we may find the same organism. Five to six food chains are thus interlinked, forming a **Food Web** and establishing a network between various species. This maintains the stability of the ecosystem. The more the number of alternative pathways the more stable is the community of organisms. Food chains are of two types, **grazing** and **detritus** food chains. A grazing food chain starts with the producers, the plants and a detritus food chain start with decayed matter called the detritus. The dead organic matter is decomposed by microorganisms. Detritivores are the primary consumers of a detritus food chain such as bacteria and fungi. A grazing food chain starts with green plants forming the first trophic level and is dependent on solar energy. The detritus food chain, however, meets its energy requirement by the degradation of dead organic matter or detritus and is directly not dependent on solar energy. Fallen leaves of plants and dead organic material form the first level of a detritus food chain. These are decomposed by microbes that feed on detritus called the detritivores or decomposers and are heterotrophs that obtain their nutrients by consuming detritus.

A grazing food chain can be:

Grasses > Grasshopper > Small birds > Hawks

A detritus food chain can be:

Dead leaves > Woodlice > Black birds

Microorganisms act as decomposers and are vital for a food chain. Decomposers break down dead plants and animals turning them into nutrients that can be used by plants. They are important to the food chain as they help recycle nutrients back into the system. In the absence of microbes these nutrients would remain locked in organic matter and plants would not be able to use them. This can disrupt the food chain as plants would not be able to grow and support the organisms that feed on them. Energy flows in an ecosystem in one direction that is unidirectionally showing that in an ecosystem the energy harnessed by autotrophs, does not return to the sun. The energy transfer follows Lindemann's law of ten percent, 1942 which states that only 10% of energy is transferred from one trophic level to another in an ecosystem. The rest is utilized for other metabolic processes and is released as heat. For example, if the producers have 100000 J, the next trophic level will be passed 10% of energy, which is 10,000 J and so on. The second law of thermodynamics states that during energy transformation, a portion of energy is dispersed into the environment as heat energy. Thus, in an ecosystem some amount of solar energy is trapped by autotrophs during photosynthesis to form food, the chemical energy,the rest of the energy is dispersed as heat during respiration and other processes.

There are two types of energy flow models:
- The **Single Channel** Energy Flow Model that illustrates that flow of energy is in a unidirectional manner within an ecosystem.
- The second is the **Two Channel** energy flow model represented as Y. One arm of the Y- represents the grazing food chain and the other arm represents the detritus food chain. The first level of the food chain is represented by different kinds of organisms at both the arms. One arm of Y represents the autotrophs whereas the other arm represents the dead decayed matter. According to this model under

natural conditions food chains are not isolated and confirms the basic stratified structure of the ecosystem.

Ecosystem is thus, a self-sustaining and stable unit and functions due to the process of energy flow within its living component.

The second function of the ecosystem is **Cycling of Nutrients** . Essential nutrients like carbon, nitrogen and phosphorus circulate through ecosystems via biological, chemical and geological processes. Cycling of nutrients in an ecosystem starts when plants absorb nutrients from the atmosphere and soil for sustaining productivity and growth in an ecosystem. Nutrients are cycled and recycled by the cyclic processes that regulate the movement of elements and their transformation within the ecosystems and the earth's environment that has the three components atmosphere, hydrosphere, and the biosphere. These nutrient cycles are also called biogeochemical cycles. The nutrients present in the soil and atmosphere are recycled, transferred into a variety of forms and re-utilized. Plants and animals utilize these nutrients. These are then released back into the environment by breaking down of dead decayed matter forming new substances or nutrients that are available to green plants for synthesis of more nutrients. Decomposers return the nutrients into the soil or oceans and are used by producers to start a new food chain. The cycle is repeated, and the flow of nutrients continues within the ecosystem in a cyclic manner. The biogeochemical cycles or the nutrient cycles are basically of three types: **gaseous, sedimentary** and **hydrologic.** Gaseous cycles are those in which the reservoir is the earth's atmosphere. Carbon,Oxygen and Nitrogen cycles are the gaseous cycles. Sedimentary cycles are those in which some nutrients are lost from the cycle and get locked into the sediments deep in the earth's crust. These are, therefore, unavailable for immediate cycling. Sulphur and Phosphorus cycles are the sedimentary cycles. Hydrologic cycle constitutes the Water cycle.

Water Cycle

Water is present on earth in oceans, on land and in the atmosphere. Our earth is called a blue planet due to the abundance of water. About 70 percent of earth's surface is covered with water, however,very little water is available for human consumption as most water is saline.Water moves continuously within the earth and the atmosphere. The water cycle shows this continuous movement of water.

It is a cycle that involves evaporation, condensation and precipitation. Evaporation of water into vapors, condensation to form clouds and precipitation back to earth in the form of rain and snow takes place in a cyclic manner. Water moves through the atmosphere across land in different phases. Heat of the sun melts the snow and glaciers to form liquid water. This water goes into the soil and from there to the plants. It then evaporates from them into the atmosphere by transpiration. Warm water vapors rise in the atmosphere where the cold air causes it to turn back into liquid form making clouds. The clouds become saturated with water and result in precipitation or rainfall. This is the process of condensation. Rain leads to filling of water bodies and thus, the process starts all over again and the water cycle continues.

Carbon Cycle

Carbon cycle is a process that moves the carbon from the atmosphere to the plants, to animals, to land that is soil and ocean through various biochemical and physical processes in a cycle such as during photosynthesis, weathering of rocks, burning of fossil fuels and volcanism. All these processes release essential elements, making them available for biological uptake, a process by which the biotic component of the ecosystem absorbs carbon dioxide from the atmosphere. Burning of fossil fuels (oil, natural gas and coal) by anthropogenic activities releases the stored carbon into the atmosphere, making it a greenhouse gas. This affects the carbon cycle. Carbon dioxide is also naturally released by decomposition of plants and animals. If there is too little carbon dioxide and other greenhouse gases, the earth would be frozen and if too much then the atmosphere may become a furnace.

Nitrogen Cycle

Air has approximately 78% nitrogen gas. However, nitrogen cannot be used by many organisms in this form, and it is fixed, decayed, nitrified and then denitrified through the nitrogen cycle. Microbes play a major role in all these four processes during recycling of nitrogen through the biosphere. The processes by which nitrogen is fixed in the atmosphere include, Lightning (atmospheric), microbes (biological) or through industrial fixation under pressure and high temperature to form ammonia. Fixation is followed by breakdown of excretory and decayed products into ammonia by microbes. Ammonia is converted into nitrates by autotrophic bacteria called nitrifying bacteria, through a process called nitrification and can be taken up directly by plants through their roots. Nitrates and nitrites are reduced by denitrification. Some of the intermediate compounds that are formed in the process are nitric oxide, nitrous oxide, and nitrous acid. Bacteria living deep in soil and ocean sediments use nitrates for their respiration.

Oxygen Cycle

In the oxygen cycle oxygen is exchanged between atmosphere, biosphere and hydrosphere. Algae present in the water bodies can release large amounts of oxygen for organisms. They produce 30-50 percent of net global oxygen important for respiration.

Oxygen is released in the atmosphere by green plants during the process of photosynthesis and is used for respiration by living beings. They inhale free oxygen and exhale carbon dioxide back into the atmosphere. Plants reuse the released carbon dioxide during photosynthesis and thus, balance the quantity of oxygen in the atmosphere. Oxygen is important for processes like combustion, breathing and decomposition. Thus, this cycle maintains the level of oxygen in the atmosphere.

Sulphur cycle

All living organisms contain sulphur. Some proteins, hormones and vitamins in all organisms have sulphur as an important constituent. Sulphur cycles between atmosphere, lithosphere, and hydrosphere. Its major reservoir is the sedimentary rocks in the lithosphere. It enters the atmosphere from natural sources such as active volcanoes and by decay of organic matter. The combustion of coal and oil for electricity production and smelting of metals also provide sources of sulphur dioxide to the atmosphere. Sulphur is an essential nutrient for plants as it improves the plant root environment. It is released when weathering of rocks takes place. In air, it is converted into sulphate. Plants and microbes take up sulphates and convert it into organic forms. It is an important cycle because it balances the concentration of Sulphur, in different reservoirs.

Phosphorus Cycle

Phosphorus cycle is also a sedimentary cycle. In this cycle phosphorus, a slow-moving element, moves through rocks, water, soil, sediments and the organisms. Phosphorus moves from deposits present on land and sediments to living beings and then to soil and water. During weathering of rocks phosphate ions and other minerals are released. Animals take the inorganic phosphate from soil. When the bodies of organisms decay after death organic phosphate is returned to soil and is available to plants. Bacteria help in breakdown of organic matter to inorganic forms of phosphorus. Overtime phosphorus in soil reaches oceans and gets incorporated into sediments. However, most of the phosphorus is locked in rocks and sediments. Phosphate fertilizers replenish the soil phosphorus.

Soil is important in nutrient cycling as it stores and moderates the release of elements and cycling of nutrients. A nutrient cycle is said to be perfect if the nutrients that are replaced are utilized also at the same pace. These cycles are continuous, and nutrients are passed repeatedly through living organisms and back into the environment. The mechanism by which changes in one component within a cycle influence other components are referred to as

Feedback. This results in either an increase or decrease in response to the initial change. Feedback can be positive or negative respectively. Positive feedback can lead to a rapid downward effect that accelerates and results in change in the system, whereas negative feedback occurs when a change results in triggering a reaction that may either oppose or neutralize the initial change. This maintains an equilibrium and thus, results in stability. The capacity of an ecosystem to maintain internal stability and equilibrium due to external fluctuations or disturbances is referred to as homoeostasis. This is important for the sustainability of earth's ecosystem that includes its diverse biodiversity. Anthropogenic activities such as land use changes, overuse of resources and pollution are a challenge to this equilibrium and can have an adverse effect on nutrient cycles.

Ecosystem services

These are the various services that man derives from ecosystems. **Millennium Ecosystem Assessment** (MA) is a UN sponsored report. Its main objective is to evaluate the effects of human activities on ecosystems. It has identified four types of ecosystem services. These are **provisioning, regulating, cultural**, and **supporting services.**

Provisioning services include production of food, water, fiber, and other resources provided by ecosystems.

Regulating services include the control of climate, air-quality, soil quality, carbon sequestration, flood regulation, pollination and pest management.

Supporting services such as nutrient cycles, oxygen release, formation of soil and provision of habitat for all organisms.

Cultural services include recreational services, such as camping, hiking, fishing, Ecotourism, and religious services.

Ecosystems play a significant role in regulating the earth's climate by influencing weather patterns through processes like evaporation and transpiration. Climate and weather patterns affect ecosystems significantly. Temperature, precipitation, and seasonal changes affect plant growth, animal behavior, and species distribution in an ecosystem. Climate phenomena like El Nino and La Nino have global impact causing shifts in weather patterns that can lead to droughts, floods, and other extreme events affecting ecosystems.

Ecosystems are also habitat for diverse species and support biodiversity by enabling complex interactions among organisms such as competition, parasitism, predation, mutualism, and commensalism. These interactions can be positive or negative.

Competition: organisms compete for the same resources such as food, water and habitat. It can be between two different types of species for the same resource.

Parasitism: relationship between two species in which one organism is benefited at the expense of the other(host). Parasites may influence host behavior.

Predation: when one organism preys on another. This is a key mechanism for controlling population and maintaining ecological balance.

Mutualism: when both species benefit from the interaction, it is called mutualism.

Commensalism: in this one organism is benefited by the other and the other is neither benefited nor harmed.

Human Impact on Ecosystems

1. **Deforestation and habitat fragmentation:** The main causes are human activities such as logging, agriculture and urbanization. These activities lead to loss of biodiversity, disruption of nutrient cycles, climate change, and increased greenhouse gas emissions.

2. **Pollution:** Emissions from industrial activities and transportation impact the air-quality affecting respiratory health and contributing to acid rain . Water pollution from contamination due to chemicals released in water bodies from industries result in eutrophication, loss of aquatic life and health hazards for man and wildlife. Soil pollution from industrial waste, pesticides, and heavy metals degrade the soil quality impacting plant growth and soil organisms.

3. **Climate change, Global Warming**: Effect species distribution , the timing of biological events and increased extinction rates.

Ecosystems adapt to climate change by nature based solutions called EbA (ecosystem-based adaptation). These include management activities for diverse ecosystems, increasing their resilience to climate change, such as sustainable management of forests, grasslands and wetlands.

Conservation efforts and sustainable practices help protect biodiversity and ecosystems. Implementing practices that minimize environmental impact like organic farming, crop rotation and selective logging. Community involvement for conservation and promoting awareness about sustainable use of natural resources as well as protection of the global ecosystems will be helpful .Conservation challenges like Human Wildlife conflict, Habitat loss, Climate change, Pollution, Overuse of resources have been deterring progress in protection and restoration of ecosystems and biodiversity they are home to.

Some examples of various conservation efforts being done for different ecosystems globally are:

- Protected areas: As in India National parks such as Dudhwa National Park, Jim Corbett National Park, Banff National Park in Canada, Yellowstone National Park, USA etc.

- Biodiversity Corridors: In countries such as Canada wildlife corridors have been established to protect the biodiversity of a particular ecosystem.
- Community involvement is being done for management of forests and aquatic ecosystems like ponds and rivers.

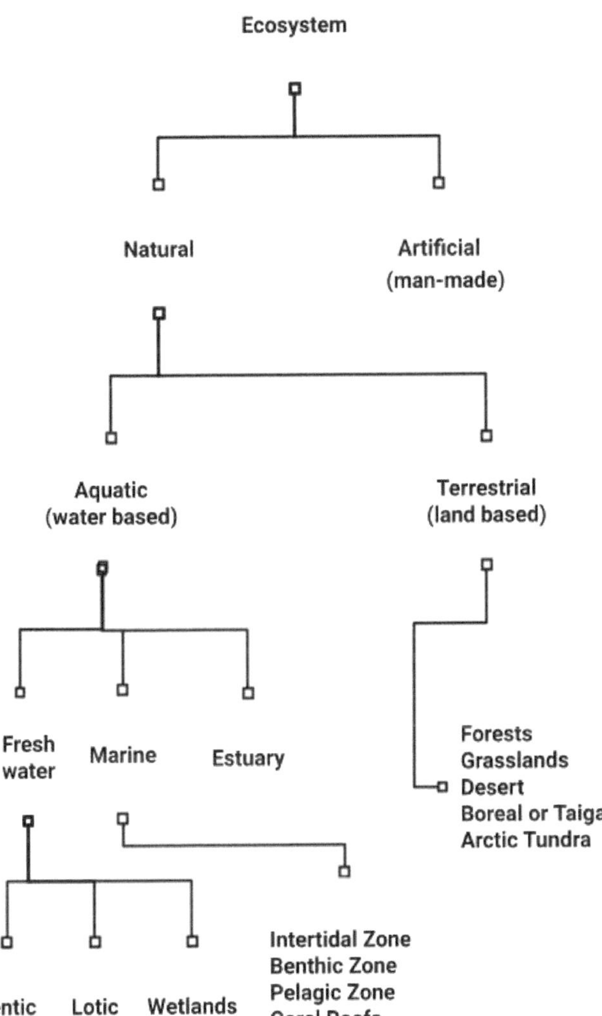

Ecosystem
Natural
Artificial (man-made)
Aquatic (water based)
Terrestrial (land based)
Fresh water
Marine
Estuary
Forests
Grasslands
Desert
Boreal or Taiga
Arctic Tundra
Lentic
Lotic
Wetlands
Intertidal Zone
Benthic Zone
Pelagic Zone
Coral Reefs

Ecosystem Types

Forest Ecosystem

Forests are terrestrial ecosystems dominated by trees growing in a closed canopy. The energy from the sun enters the system through producers that can photosynthesize and produce food. Huge trees make a forest that are spaced far apart and beneath. The main canopy has closely spaced trees. These trees provide fruits, nectar, seeds for many primary consumers.

The understory supports few plants as it receives less sunlight.Forest ecosystems are home to a vast variety of fauna and tree species specific to the ecosystem.

Forest ecosystem are of three types:

- Tropical rainforest
- Temperate rainforest
- Boreal or Taiga forest

Tropical Rainforests: These occur in regions with hot humid climate and high annual rainfall(average being 70 inches). They are located near the equator, mainly in the South and Central America (Amazon basin), Africa (Congo basin), S.E Asia and tropical Australia.

These areas have consistent warm temperatures (25-30 deg C) all year. Soil conditions vary with location and climate. Structurally, tropical rainforests are very complex and house about 50 percent of all plant and animal species present on Earth.Plants with similar stage and lifeform are grouped into a category called Synusiae that make up a distinct layer of vegetation. These are present more in such ecosystems than any other type. The plants of this layer are self-supporting. Saprophytic, parasitic and epiphytic species are common. Palms, banana trees, ferns and orchids are a few examples of flora of the tropical rain forests.

Tropical deciduous forest is also known as tropical dry forests or the monsoon forests.The trees have broad leaves due to consistent rainfall. These forests adapt to dry periods by shedding leaves leading to open canopy and are, therefore, called tropical deciduous forests. The climate in such forests is a long dry season and the trees shed their leaves in this season followed by a period of heavy rainfall when the leaves regrow.Climate supports diverse plant species such as oak,maple,aspen teak, bamboos etc. and Fauna such as large cats, monkeys, birds etc.The Amazon rainforest is home to a semi aquatic rodent Capybara, a primary consumer that feeds on grasses and forage. The main difference between tropical deciduous forests and tropical rainforest is response to seasonal rainfall.

Temperate Forest: They are characterized by broad leaves and coniferous trees that have needle-like leaves. Northern and Southern hemisphere temperate forests are quite different from each other.

The temperate forests are found in regions like North America, Europe and East Asia. In the Southern Hemisphere the temperate forests occur in New Zealand and Tasmania (Australia).

They receive moderate rainfall between 30 to 60 inches annually. The average daily temperatures range from -30°C to 30°C experiencing cold winters and warm summers. In the temperate forests of the southern hemisphere warm and mild climatic conditions are often seen.

The temperate forests are of two types deciduous and evergreen. East North America, East Asia and West Europe have deciduous temperate forests with moist warm summers and frosty winters. Oak, birches, and maple are some of the dominant trees in mid latitude deciduous forest. The evergreen coniferous forest has mild frost-free winters. They may have broad leaves and sclerophyllous forests. In sclerophyllous the vegetation has small, hard and thick leaves. Soil is poor in mineral nutrients. They are found in areas with low and irregular rainfall as in Australia and the Mediterranean region. Broad leaved temperate forests have all year-round rainfall. The soil is fertile with high levels of organic matter. Richness of ground flora below the trees increases soil fertility. The broad-leaved forests are present in New Zealand, East Australia, South America, South China, Korea, and Japan. The evergreen Coniferous temperate forest has pines, spruce and fir trees. They support diverse animal species, such as deer, bears, wolves, and numerous bird species.

Boreal or Taiga Forests: These occupy around 17 percent of the earth's land surface and are in northern latitudes from Canada to Alaska to Russia to Scandinavia. The Southern Hemisphere does not have boreal forests. Boreal forests are characterized by long dry cold winters and short mild summers. Snow cover is persistent for much of the year. They have short growing seasons. In summers, the mean annual temperature ranges, from slightly above freezing to as low as -10°C with coldest as -50°C in winters. Soil is acidic and nutrient poor, these forests experience very little precipitation.

Boreal forests are evergreen, though they have a limited number of plant species adapted to the cold climate and short growing seasons. Ground cover has grasses, mosses and lichens. The forests are dominated by cold tolerant, and fire adapted, Coniferous trees as Pines (Pinus), spruce (Picea), fir (Abies) and Larches (Larix), tall shrubs, such as Pine cherry, alder, hazel and Mountain ash.

Broadleaf deciduous trees, such as balsam poplar, aspen are also common in these forests. Wide variety of wildlife like large mammals (moose, black bears), small mammals (red squirrel, hares) and birds (owls and woodpeckers) are common. Wolf and lynx are major predators in a boreal forest. The primary decomposers are the microbes, bacteria and fungi.

The main natural and anthropogenic events that disturb such forest areas are climate change, woodland fires, pest infestation, forestry, resource and urban development.

Grassland Ecosystem

Grasslands are open areas of land where grasses are the dominant species. Trees are rare to observe. These are found in regions with moderate rainfall and have seasonal variations in both temperature and precipitation.

The two major types of grasslands are tropical and temperate grasslands. The regions in which grasslands are present, have hot summers and low precipitation. Tropical Savanna grassland occurs in Africa, Asia, Australia and South America. The Prairies of North America, Steppes in Eurasia extending from Hungary to China, Pampas of

Argentina, Downs of Australia and New Zealand have temperate grasslands. The smallest grassland in the world is the African Madagascan montane grassland and shrubland.

Grassland ecosystems are influenced by the biotic community, local climate, the natural landscape and natural disturbances such as fires and floods. Most of the world's large animals live in grasslands. They support large herbivores like bison, zebras, and antelopes, along with their predators like wolves and lions. The one horned rhinoceros is one of the threatened grassland animals in the north-east region of India. Jaguar, African wild dog,

African elephant, Indian elephant are some of the other species present in grasslands.

Grasslands of the world:

- **Steppes**: These are dry, grassy plains without any trees and occur in temperate regions of the world, mainly east Europe and central Asia (Eurasia) stretching to neighboring countries like Russia, Kazakhstan. They receive 10 to 12 inches of rain annually. Wolves, foxes, Falcons, and eagles are commonly found here.

- **Pampas**: These are fertile South American low-temperature grasslands that cover a vast area. They extend to Argentina, all of Uruguay and southern Brazil. More than 400 species of birds and about hundred species of terrestrial mammals are found here. The Greater Rhea is the largest of birds of these open grasslands and is like emus and ostriches in being flightless with long legs.

- **Velds**: These are temperate grasslands of South Africa.They have a mild climate with cold and dry winters . Temperature ranges between 5°C to 10°C .The months from May to September are winters with July being the coldest . The soil is not very fertile as they do not receive much rain. The prominent fauna are lions, leopards, cheetahs, giraffes, and antelopes. The natural vegetation is grasses and some bushes with scattered trees at higher elevations.

- **Downs**: These are temperate grasslands found in Australia. They have the richest soil in the world. Summers are hot and winters cold due to elevation. Average annual temperature is 19°C.

The vegetation is mostly grasses, wildflowers, low shrubs and scattered Acacia trees. Kangaroo is the main animal found in Australian downs, however dingoes, koala, platypus are also seen.

- **Prairies**: These are the grasslands of North America, lowlands of Canada, Mexico that include all the great Plains as well as wetter, hilly lands. They extend from the Rocky Mountains to east of the Mississippi river and from Saskatchewan in Canada to Texas in the US.

Besides grasses, they also contain shrubs but have very few trees. The prairies with tall grasses receive about 30 inches of rain per year, whereas prairies with short grasses receive about 12 inches of rain annually. The common grasses are wheat grass and spear grass. They experience moderate temperature and rainfall, however, in the majority of prairie areas, snowy humid continental climates with cool summers are observed. The summers are short, and warm winters are very cold. A thick blanket of snow may cover some regions of Prairies in Canada and the US. Tall trees up to 2 m high such as willows, alders and poplar grow in areas having water. The American buffalo or bison is the main fauna of Prairie. Rabbits, dogs, coyotes and gophers are also common in these grasslands.

- **Savannas**: These are tropical or subtropical grasslands. They have scattered trees above a layer of grasses that are tall and continuous. They cover more than half of Africa and vast areas of South

America, Australia and India. They have a hot seasonal dry climate. Rainfall occurs a few months annually. The mean annual precipitation ranges from 20-60 inches with a longer dry season. The Savanna can be wet, dry or thorn bush type. In all seasons the climate is warm and hot with an average temperature of 10 to 20°C in the dry season and 20 to 30°C in the wet season. The wct Savanna has dry seasons lasting 3 to 5 months, whereas in dry Savana it is longer, extending from 5 to 7 months. Thorn bush Savannas have an even longer dry season. In Savannas the soil is less fertile. The Savanna of Asia and tropical America have some rainforests nearer to the equator with deciduous broad-leaved trees that shed leaves during the dry season. Cut grass, Bahia grass, succulents such as Euphorbia are common. Prosopis is a common woody plant of South America. Wide diversity of spy shrubs, grasses like kangaroo grass, bluestem grass are common in dry Savannas. In the wet savannas Brachystegia trees grow above an understory of elephant grass (Pennisetum purpureum). Indian Savanna commonly consists of Thorny trees of Acacia, Mimosa and Ziziphus. In

Australia, the grasslands resemble the sclerophyllous vegetation that is characterized by hard leathery evergreen foliage. Most Australian trees in Savanna grasslands are evergreen and they survive the dry season, not by dropping their leaves, but by reducing water loss from them. Various species of Eucalyptus, Acacia are also common. Savannas provide habitat for diverse fauna that maintain them by grazing. Grasshoppers, caterpillars and termites are very common. Large mammals, such as zebra, rhinoceros, hippopotamus, and antelope also form the biotic community of these grasslands. The Savannas of Africa have lions,gazelles and elephants.

Desert Ecosystem

Deserts are regions with extremely low precipitation and have little vegetation. They are characterized by arid conditions resulting in availability of less moisture to plants for growth. This is due to improper balance between rainfall and evaporation. High daytime temperatures and winds with low atmospheric humidity, make the conditions more severe for any plant growth. Average annual precipitation ranges from 0 to about 1 inch.

Deserts are classified based on their climate and geography into two: hot deserts and cold deserts.

- Hot deserts have very high temperatures during daytime, mainly in summers. In all hot deserts maximum temperature exceeds 40°C. In deserts of Libya a maximum temperature of 58°C has been recorded. Soil surface temperature can even rise to 78°C as recorded in the hot desert Sahara. Night temperatures, however, fall fast. Minimum temperatures are generally below freezing point. Mean annual temperatures lie between 20 to 25°C.

Sahara, Arabian Kalahari and Sonoran are the hot deserts of the world.

- The cold deserts are found in temperate regions at higher altitudes. As they are away from the coast, atmospheric humidity is less and are devoid of onshore winds. The cold deserts experience colder temperatures, especially in winters.

Central Asia has the largest area of temperate deserts. Western North America, South-east South America and South Australian deserts have smaller areas. The main cold deserts of the world are Gobi in northern China and southern Mongolia, Atacama in Northern Chile in South America and the polar deserts of Antarctica and Arctic.

Ladakh is a cold desert of India in the Himalayan region. These cold deserts receive very little precipitation, mostly in the form of snow or fog.

Desert soils are mostly alkaline sandy or gravel, loam or shallow stony soils. These soils may support microbial communities. The main flora of deserts are the thorny plants, prickly saltwort and the daisies. Smaller shrubs like

Artemisia and Ephedra are present in central Asia and North American deserts. Perennial grasses are most common in deserts. Cupressus and Pinus trees are found in some deserts. The fauna of deserts is regionally distinct. Australian deserts have high diversity of reptiles, few mammals like the marsupials that include a wide range of kangaroos, wallabies, bandicoots, European rabbits. Donkeys, goats, sheep, and horses are domesticated. Foxes, hyena, and many cat family species, like leopards and lynx are common. Finches and pigeons are the common birds of deserts.

Underground organs, such as bulbs, tubers, rhizomes help desert plants to survive dry periods. These structures are inactive. They use little water and grow in very less moisture conditions. Water storage organs, such as succulent stems of cacti, hold water until it is needed. Leaves are of reduced size. Some of the desert flora have dormant seeds that germinate as soon as some favorable conditions such as rain is available, the plants grow and complete their life cycle in a very short period and are called ephemeral plants that are short-lived plants.

Desert animals also have adaptations to survive the infrequent moisture availability. These animals remain underground in burrows where the climate is cool and humid during dry periods. For example snails may remain dormant for long periods. In deserts, the productivity is very low and varies from time to time.

Tundra Ecosystems

Tundra ecosystems are found in polar regions, including the arctic circle in Alaska, Canada, Russia, Greenland, Iceland and Scandinavia. High altitudes of alpine areas have tundra ecosystems all around the world. Antarctica is covered with ice all over and lacks well developed tundra. The climate of the tundra region is extremely cold, dry and windy. It may get warm in the summer months that are not more than two months in a year. Rainfall is very less. Most of the year the area is covered with snow. They have very short growing seasons and have low biodiversity. It has long stretched barc ground, and rocks with patchy vegetation. Lichens, mosses, herbs, and small shrubs are common. In summers many wildflowers are seen growing. The tundra region due to its harsh climatic conditions is a treeless plain. The fauna of tundra includes arctic foxes, Caribou and migratory birds. The presence of Permafrost is essential to all life in this region, as it is habitat for many of the fauna living in this ecosystem. Permafrost is persistently frozen ground below the topsoil over much of the arctic and extends to depths of 350 to 650 m. Alternate freezing and thawing of ground is common in tundra region, thus separating it from the adjacent ecosystems, the evergreen taiga and polar barrens. The arctic tundra is the coldest, encircling the north pole and extending as far as the northern taiga belt where coniferous forests begin. Downward movement of water through the soil is delayed or slowed due to formation of permafrost making lowlands of the arctic region boggy during summers and during the winters, water in the soil freezes into ice. The amount of snow in the alpine tundra is more than the arctic tundra. Rapid drainage is observed in Alpine tundra due to the steep hilly topography.

Climate of the Tundra region varies considerably, and the most severe climate is seen in the arctic region with a temperature fluctuation ranging from 4°C to -32°C during winters.

Alpine Tundra has a moderate climate. Summers are cool with a temperature of 3 to 12°C and winters are moderate with temperatures that might not fall below -18°C. Annual precipitation of less than 15 inches mainly in the summers, has been recorded. Snow is accumulated at higher altitudes of the arctic tundra region. Lichens, mosses and berry bearing shrubs form the common flora of the region. The fauna includes distinct species like the seals, polar bears, snow owls, muskoxen, and arctic hares. These faunae eat tundra vegetation. Wolves and arctic foxes are the tertiary consumers.

Snow geese and Canada geese are two large birds that live in the wild climate of tundra. Human activities like hunting, oil drilling, infrastructure development have altered the landscape and are a threat to wildlife of the area. Melting of glaciers and permafrost is a threat to this ecosystem as it can release carbon into the atmosphere. Average temperatures of the area are rising fast due to climate change. Shrub density, migration of species are some of the consequences faced due to the change in the climate.

Aquatic Ecosystems

These are water-based ecosystems and are of three main types:

- Freshwater
- Marine
- Estuaries

They are home to diverse species of plants, fishes and crustaceans.

Freshwater Ecosystems

These have low dissolved salt concentrations. The freshwater ecosystems, are of three types:

- Lentic
- Lotic
- Wetland

Lentic Freshwater Ecosystem

The term Lentic comes from the Latin Word *lentus* meaning slow or standing water bodies like ponds and lakes. These ecosystems do not have any downhill flow. Some lakes are permanent, for example, deep, rift, lakes of Africa, and Asia whereas others are ephemeral and retain water for a few weeks only. These occur on all continents, except Antarctica.

Lakes cover 4,200,000 m² of the area worldwide. They occur in every continent but are concentrated in the northern hemisphere. Natural lakes are formed in many ways, for example by landslides, glaciers, tectonic, and volcanic activities and less violent action of rivers, etc.

The Lentic ecosystem has several abiotic zones. The division is based on the distance from the shore, light penetration and temperature change. The zone that extends downwards where sunlight can penetrate is the photic zone and inhabits most primary producers and consumers. Below these depths is the aphotic zone. The region near the shore where rooted macrophytes are present is called the littoral zone. It is a shallow, photic zone. The entire open water area is located away from the shore and the littoral zone and is called the limnetic zone or pelagic zone. The benthic zone is another abiotic zone of the lentic ecosystem. It is further subdivided into categories. Most lakes in temperate zones become stratified with a layer of lighter water, the epilimnion, an uppermost and warmest layer of a lake. It floats over the denser hypolimnion which is the deepest and coldest layer of a thermally stratified lake. Thermal stratification of the lake is dependent on seasons. These two zones are separated by a layer the metalimnion where change in temperature occurs rapidly. The boundary between the epilimnion and the hypolimnion is called thermocline. Rapid temperature change occurs here depending on the depth. Very less exchange of water occurs between epilimnion and hypolimnion during stratification. The concentration of chemicals and pH varies.

The biotic community of lakes is the invertebrates like Zooplankton (protozoa, Rotifers) within water and benthos that live in or on just above the bottom often together with macrophytes. Other organisms in lakes can be cyanobacteria, littoral zone fleas, submerged macrophytes etc. Sedges are common in saline lakes. Epiphytic algae colonize submerged and emergent plants. Benthic algae such as Chara and Oedogonium are present in lakes that cover the littoral zone. Plants such as macrophytes live in both benthic and pelagic zones. Bacteria are present in all regions of lentic waters.

Lotic Freshwater Ecosystem

The term Lotic comes from the Latin word *lotus* that refers to running water. Lotic ecosystems are faster, moving water bodies like streams and rivers and are important biologically. The water flows in a downhill direction.

Rivers are free flowing open freshwater Lotic ecosystems that are affected by external factors. They flow free from the headquarters and throughout the entire watershed travel downstream. The steepness of the slope impacts the speed of water flow and the size of particles, such as silt, pebbles that can settle to the stream bed. The force of moving water pushes the larger stones, and even Boulders.

When the speed of water decreases, the larger pebbles drop, and smaller ones travel further downstream. Minerals that have been dissolved from the land also flow through the river waters. The type and concentration of minerals vary and have an impact on the type of biodiversity surviving there.

Due to continuous movement of water in Lotic ecosystems the oxygen level is much higher. The water is clearer than Lentic ecosystems. The main animals of the Lotic ecosystem are crocodiles, alligators, Dolphins, and hippos. The flora of rivers includes algae, phytoplankton etc.

Wetlands

Wetlands are land surface areas that spend at least part of their existence submerged or predominantly wet. They may both be fresh and saltwater bodies, including swamps, marshes and bogs. They vary in size and are found in coastal regions as well as inlands.

The wetlands are a highly diverse and unique habitat rich in biodiversity, supporting and providing services to the planet Earth. They are the most valuable ecosystems on the earth.

Some wetlands support endangered species that are not present elsewhere. They offer natural floodplains for rivers that expand rapidly and safeguard the neighboring communities. They harbor fish, amphibians, mollusks and crustacean nurseries. They act as nature's filters, screening pollutants from the water that flows through. They act like giant sponges or reservoirs and are sites for recreational activities.

There are three major kinds of wetland

- Swamps

- Marshes

- Bogs

Swamps

These are wetlands that are always flooded with water. They are dominated by trees. Swamps are of two types: freshwater and saltwater swamps. The freshwater swamps are generally present near lakes or streams, however, saltwater swamps are more common in coastal regions. Plants that can tolerate water such as lotus, Cypress, and cattails grow in swamps. Alligators, frogs, snakes may swim among the plants that are present in the swamps. The saltwater swamps are generally present in areas where the soil surface is covered by sea water at the time of tides near coastlines in tropics. Mangroves are common in such swamps. These plants have roots above the ground called peg or prop roots. These roots filter pollutants from the water. These swamps are also home to a variety of birds. The roots of mangroves are resting sites for these birds. Sea birds like seagulls and heron are present in saltwater swamps. The largest mangrove forest of the world, the Sundarbans is present in India and parts of Bangladesh. Algae and mosses are common flora in these mangrove forests. Palms and grasses grow in dry areas of the swamp. Fauna like bees, storks, and heron are found in these swamps. Many fishes inhabit this area, forming food for birds. Birds like Kingfisher and pigeons roost in shrubs of this area. Crabs and shrimps are common. Large reptiles, prey mammals like deer, bear, mongooses, and monkeys are common in Sunderbans. Bengal tiger, an endangered species, is also common in these mangroves.

Marshes

These are present near river mouths and along coastlines. They are dominated by grasses. Many aquatic plants grow in marshes. Marshes are also of two types: freshwater marshes and saltwater marshes.

The freshwater marshes are present away from coastal regions around lakes and streams. The main flora are grasses and aquatic plants such as Sawgrass and Cypress. Some of the rare orchid species also grow in these muddy waters. The main consumers are insects, fish, shrimps, alligators, deer, and dolphins.

Saltwater marshes are dominated by grasses. Shellfish, amphibians, reptiles and fishes live here and obtain their food from these marshes. Birds and insects are also common. Few mangrove trees are also present.

Bogs

These are common in cold arctic areas of North America, Europe and Asia. They form in areas where the upper surface of underground water is high. The main flora is the water loving grasses and sedges. The water of the bog is covered with a floating mat of vegetation. The decayed vegetation at the bottom of the bog forms a thick spongy mat called peat. Sphagnum moss is common in bogs, its decayed form is called peat moss. Bogs are not fertile. They have acidic soil with more water content than swamps and marshes. Nutrients like nitrogen are very low. Cranberries, blueberries can grow in bogs.Pitcher Plants and sundew are carnivorous plants that trap and consume insects, butterflies, dragonflies and are common in bogs. Larger animals are generally not found in bogs. Sometimes moose are observed that consume aquatic plants like pond lilies.

Marine Ecosystems

Marine ecosystems cover 2/3rd of the surface of the earth i.e. around 70 percent of the earth surface. They are called marine because of the high level of dissolved salts present in the water. Oceans and seas form marine ecosystems. Globally, world oceans have been divided into 66 large marine ecosystems. These ecosystems are the largest of the earth's aquatic ecosystem.

They include open ocean, the deep-sea ocean and the coastal marine ecosystems. The abiotic factors in a marine ecosystem are sunlight, temperature,oxygen and nutrients dissolved in the water.

Depending on the amount of sunlight, the marine ecosystem receive they are divided into three parts:

- The topmost part is the Euphotic zone that extends down as far as 200 m below the surface, sufficient light is available for normal photosynthetic activity at this depth. Many marine organisms are present in this region.
- The Dysphotic zone is below the euphotic zone and is 200 to 1000 m below the surface. The surface sunlight is available in this zone for some photosynthesis.
- The Aphotic zone is below the Dysphotic zone and is devoid of sunlight.

Plants like kelps, phytoplankton, seaweeds, sea grasses etc. are common in these ecosystems. Fishes like sharks, tuna, eels, seahorse, swordfish, stingray, rockfish etc. are common.

Mollusks like cuttlefish, oysters, snails, octopus, and mammals like seals, blue whales, etc. are present in marine waters.

Depending on water depth and the shoreline marine ecosystems are divided into various zones:

- The Oceanic Zone: This is a vast open part of the ocean with fauna, such as Whales, Sharks, and Tuna. The common flora is golden seaweed and Sargassum. Phytoplankton and red algae are also common in this zone of the marine ecosystem.
- The Benthic Zone: This is the deep sea and the sea floor region. Many invertebrates live in the benthic

zone. It is home to sea cucumbers, sea stars, sea urchins. Benthic fish like catfish, stingrays, hagfish, mollusks like oysters and clams are very common. Corals are present in this zone. Kelp forests and sea grasses are also common in benthic zones.

- The Intertidal Zone: These are the areas where the ocean meets the land between high and low tides. The main fauna of this region are marine snails, hermit crabs, sea stars, sea urchins and mussels. The intertidal zone has various kinds of green algae like the sea lettuce (Ulva), Codium species, seagrass and eelgrass.
- Near Shore zone (neritic): It is the zone near the shore that receives plenty of sunlight. The main flora are the seagrass meadows, plankton, algae. The animals inhabiting this zone are the protists, crabs, jelly fishes, scallops and shrimps.

Marine ecosystems are divided into several broad categories:

- Coral reefs
- The open ocean
- The deep-sea ocean

Coral Reefs

These are built from exoskeleton secreted by coral polyps. Millions of minute living creatures called polyps form the reef. Reefs are home to a diverse variety of organisms. The polyps feed on the plankton. The coral polyps depend on zooxanthellae for their metabolic processes.

The present-day reef is about 10,000 years old. The massive structures that make up the Great Barrier Reef are a complex of corals in the Pacific Ocean off the north-eastern coast of Australia. It is the longest and largest reef Complex in the world. It has an area of 350000 km² and is the largest structure built by living organisms. The reef has 2100 individual reefs and around 800 fringing reefs formed around islands or the bordering coastlines.

Some of the reefs are dry at low tide whereas some are islands of coral sands or cays. The accumulation of carbonate, sand and mud provide a habitat for sea grasses and small blue green algae mats. Beaches are formed by accumulation of sediments along the sea or lake shores.

Coral that built reefs grow best in shallow sunlit water at a depth of 36 feet. Normal saline water with high oxygen content having a mean annual temperature of 22°C- 28°C is preferred by corals. Plant nutrients like phosphate and nitrate are present. The water current and the wind both help in formation of the reefs. Phytoplankton and zooplanktons are present in these regions. Zooplanktons form the chief food supply of the corals.

Coral reefs take four forms:

- Fringing reefs

- Barrier reefs

- Atolls

- Platform

According to world famous naturalist Sir David Attenborough, the Great Barrier Reef is facing environmental challenges due to increase in ocean temperature and acidity of the water of the ocean. Coral bleaching has been recorded in oceans worldwide. Global initiatives such as coral reef monitoring networks help in monitoring the reef zones and raising public awareness. However, coral reefs maintain a diverse and complex ecosystem.

Some of the large marine ecosystems are Gulf of Mexico, Gulf of Alaska, Gulf of California, Bay of Bengal, great barrier reef, north Australian shelf, etc.

Open Ocean Systems

The open ocean systems have plenty of sunlight, warm temperature and enough oxygen. It supports fauna such as Dolphins, octopuses, sharks and whales. The main flora are seaweeds, red algae, kelps and sargassum.

Deep sea ecosystems

The Deep Sea Ecosystems are regions deep inside the oceans at its floor. They are deep, dark and cold ecosystems. Sunlight cannot penetrate till the seafloor. Light in the ocean decreases with depth. The physical environment of deep-sea oceans is very different from habitat near the surface of the ocean. It supports diverse organisms. The unusual adaptations in animals help them to survive these challenging environments. The organisms such as squids, fishes, whales, crabs, elephant seals, worms and some sharks are found in such ecosystems. Killer whales are the top predators. The main flora are the seagrasses, sargassum, red algae and phytoplankton.

Estuaries

These are areas where rivers meet the ocean. The salty ocean mixes with the freshwater of rivers. The water of an estuary is called brackish water. It can be called a bay or a lagoon. River water flows at a high speed into the sea or an ocean. Estuaries are among the most productive places on earth supporting life. They are home to some unique flora and fauna. Some of the plants found in an estuary are red algae, sea lettuce, and salt grass. The fauna present in an estuary are fishes such as salmon, sharks, other fauna are insects, crabs, shrimps, scallop, jellyfish, seal, turtles etc.

Special Reference to the
Major Ecosystems of the Globe

Ecosystems of North America

North America spans a wide range of latitudes and altitudes, resulting in diverse climate and ecosystems. The continent includes Arctic tundra in the north, temperate forests, vast grasslands, arid deserts and diverse freshwater and coastal ecosystems.

Due to its varied geography, the continent of North America supports unique flora and fauna. The boreal forests known as the Taiga extend across Canada, Alaska up to Newfoundland. They are dominated by coniferous trees like spruce, fir and pine. The forest floor is covered with mosses, lichens and shrubs. The fauna includes large mammals (moose, bear, wolves), small mammals (squirrels, hare) and a wide variety of bird species (owls, woodpeckers).

The temperate rainforests are located along the pacific northwest coast, from California to Alaska. Dense growth of evergreen trees like spruce, Douglas fir, some ferns and mosses are also present. These forests receive high annual rainfall and have unique undergrowth. Species such as black bears, bald eagles' salmon, elk are very common.

The deciduous forests are common in the Eastern US extending into Canada. These forests undergo seasonal changes. Trees like oak, maple, birch that shed leaves seasonally are present in this ecosystem. The red maple, a beautiful native tree, is most abundant in the North East of the US. A thorny tree species, the Locust tree with clustered white flowers is also native. Willow trees are also common. Diverse animal species like red foxes, white tailed deer and birds like woodpeckers are common.

Prairies are the grasslands of North America. They stretch from Canada to Mexico. These are dominated by grasses and herbs. The prairies in Illinois are a mixture of grasses and soft stemmed plants called forbs. These areas receive enough rain to support plant growth.

Big bluestem is the state prairie grass that can grow to a height of 12 feet. Fauna such as bison, wolves, coyotes and pronghorns are common. Bird species like owls and chickens are found. Squirrels and the monarch butterfly are very common in the prairies.

The major deserts of North America are the Mojave and Great Basin. Desert plants like cactus and succulents are present in these deserts. Low rainfall and extreme temperatures with day and night variations support a unique biodiversity. The various animal species that are found here are desert tortoise, kangaroo rats, jack rabbits.Kangaroo mouse in Nevada desert rarely drinks water and obtains most of its water requirements from its food .

The freshwater ecosystems of North America have many lakes, (Great lakes, Lake Tahoe and rivers such as Mississippi, Colorado, Yukon). These support a wide range of organisms like frogs, fishes, dragonflies etc. and submerged plants like bladderworts, pond weeds etc.

The Wetlands of this continent are found in Florida, Illinois and are rich in bird species like ducks, herons, waterfowls, alligators, frogs and a variety of plant species like bogs, mangrove swamps, cattails etc.

Ecosystems of Canada

Canada has a diverse range of ecosystems ranging from vast forests to grasslands to tundra to freshwater lakes. The Taiga forests cover most areas of this country. These are dominated by coniferous trees like spruce, fir and pine. Fauna like moose, lynx, wolves and black bears are very common. The temperate forests extend in the province of British Columbia. Trees such as hemlock, Douglas fir and cedars are present in this region. These temperate rainforests support species like bald eagles and grizzly bears. The deciduous forests are present in the province of Ontario and Quebec. Maple trees, oak and birch trees grow in these forests. Fauna like deer, racoons are very common.

Prairies are the grasslands of Alberta, Manitoba and Saskatchewan provinces. These are dominated by grasses and wildflower species and are home to fauna like falcons, owls, bison. The tundra ecosystem in Canada is both arctic and alpine. The arctic tundra is covered with permafrost. Due to short growing seasons short shrubs, mosses and lichens are the dominant vegetation. Wildlife such as polar bears, arctic foxes, snowy owls and caribou are found in this ecosystem. The alpine tundra constitutes the Rocky Mountains that support species adapted to cold like mountain goats.

The aquatic ecosystem is both freshwater rivers and lakes like Lake Ontario, Lake Superior etc. Canada has many lakes and rivers that support diverse aquatic life. The marine ecosystem of Canada is formed by the Atlantic, Arctic and Pacific oceans supporting fauna such as lobsters, cod, salmon. Polar bears and seals also inhabit this ecosystem. Kelp forests support the fauna. Canada Boreal ecosystems have started facing the challenges from climate change. Conservation efforts by making protected areas, wildlife corridors are all in progress.

Ecosystems of Australia

Australia's unique geographic position and climatic variations have led to development of diverse ecosystems in this vast continent . From tropical rain forests to arid deserts to the Great Barrier Reef with coral reefs to the vast Savannas, the grasslands. These diverse ecosystems make the continent of Australia resilient and adaptable for supporting a wide variety of species.

The rainforests of Australia cover a small part of this country . They are tropical, subtropical and temperate. The rain forests of the wet tropics of Australia, a world heritage area, are found in Queensland called the Daintree Rainforest. These are dominated by evergreen trees, ferns and epiphytes. Ferns such as the King Ferns, Fan Palms are common. The ancient gymnosperm, a living fossil Wollemi Pine, is also present in these forests. The dense canopy creates a humid environment. As observed, pockets of primitive plants have remained undisturbed here for many years.

They are home to a diverse range of species including tree kangaroos, various reptiles and amphibians. The Daintree rainforest of Australia is one of the oldest and beautiful rainforests in the world .The Kuranda railway journey takes us through the lush green canopies, deep gorges and rugged mountains before reaching the Barron falls, an unforgettable 90 minute passage amidst the forests before reaching the Kuranda station that itself looks like a botanical garden .The sky rail, the longest gondola cableway in the world gives a birds eye view covering a distance of 7.5 km over the top of the rainforest, just a meters above the treetops of the world heritage site - Barron Gorge National Park.

The temperate rain forests of Australia are present in parts of the state of Victoria and Tasmania. These are dominated by tall eucalyptus trees, mosses and ferns. The forests receive high rainfall and have cool, temperate climate. The main fauna are the marsupials, lyrebirds.

Grasslands, the Savannas are found in the north of Australia particularly in the tropical regions of Queensland, the Northern Territory and Western Australia. These areas have a tropical climate with both wet and dry seasons. They are dominated by grasses with scattered trees of Eucalyptus and acacia shrubs that support many herbivores like kangaroos and wallabies as well as dingoes, birds, reptiles and insects.

The deserts of Australia cover about 18 percent of the continent and include the Great Victoria Desert, Simpson desert, Gibson desert, Great Sandy desert and a few more. The Great Victoria Desert is the largest in the continent and is known for red sand dunes, salt lakes. These experience extremely low rainfall and high temperature between day and night. Plants such as saltbush, spinifex and grass adapted to sandy soils are common. These are adapted to store water. Animals like the red kangaroos, thorny devil, a lizard with spiny skin to collect water, other reptiles and birds like emu survive in these harsh conditions.

The aquatic ecosystems of Australia are diverse and include freshwater rivers, lakes, wetlands and marine and coastal regions. The major water bodies include the Murray-Darling River system and supports diverse species like Murray cod, amphibians and other invertebrates. The Great Barrier Reef is located in Far North Queensland in Australia. It is in the list of UNESCO World Heritage Sites. It is not one reef but a collection of about 3000 individual reefs of various sizes present at variable distances from the mainland. The large colorful reefs form an intricate ecosystem. It is a home to many flora and fauna found in the world. These are turtles, jelly fishes, crocodiles and other marine creatures including soft and hard corals, whales, Dolphins, sharks and a variety of mollusks.

The mangroves are found along the northern and eastern coasts of Australia's extensive coastline and support a variety of fishes, crustaceans and birds. They provide nurseries for fish and protect from soil erosion. Estuaries like Moreton Bay are important for migratory birds and marine life.

Australia has the world's largest Seagrass beds. These provide habitat to green sea turtles and dugongs. The shark bay, another UNESCO World Heritage site, has these seagrass meadows. Australia also has the temperate marine ecosystems that are home to brown algal kelp forests in its Tasmania state. Sea dragons and fur seals are found in this ecosystem. Little penguins are also found along southern coasts.

The open ocean surrounding Australia supports a wide range of marine life like large fishes, sharks, seabirds and marine mammals. A continent with a vast and diverse natural beauty has some of the threatened and unique fauna like the whale sharks, humpback whales, blue ringed octopuses.

Ecosystems of India

India has a diverse geography and climate. It ranges from the Himalayas in the north to the tropical forests of the south and from the Thar Desert in the west to the Sundarbans in the east. This diversity results in a wide variety of ecosystems each with unique characteristics and species diversity.

The forests in India are tropical, deciduous as well as coniferous. The tropical are present in western ghats, NE states, Andaman and Nicobar Islands. They are dense forests with high rainfall and have fauna such as Asian elephants, tigers etc. The coniferous in the Himalayan region and are home to snow leopards and yaks. They are dominated by trees. The deciduous forests are common in central India and western Ghats. These host species like leopards, Bengal Tigers and deer.

The grasslands are distributed in the deccan plateau, parts of Gujarat and regions of Rajasthan. The Terai region also has vast grasslands. It is present in the Himalayan foothills known for its fertile plains' spreads in the states of Uttarakhand, Uttar Pradesh and West Bengal. It also includes parts of Nepal. These regions have a semi-arid to tropical climate with dry periods and seasonal heavy monsoonal rainfall. Winters are dry. They are dominated by grasses such as the elephant grass. Some trees such as the Sal tree are also present in these grasslands. They support consumers such as blackbuck, nilgai, lions, Indian leopards and various birds.

The major desert ecosystem of India is the Thar desert. It is a dry, arid ecosystem with very low rainfall and extreme temperatures. It is characterized by vast sand dunes, rocky terrains and very little vegetation. Thorny plants such as cacti, acacia are common. Grasses like Cenchrus sp. are found in these deserts. Fauna such as reptiles, camels, rodents, Indian gazelle [chinkara], desert fox and the critically endangered bird species Great Indian Bustard are part of this ecosystem.

Ladakh is a cold desert of India in the great Himalayan region.The desert has white sand .It is home to many animals such as Himalayan brown bear, Snow Leopard, Tibetan wild ass and double humped camels. Birds like black necked cranes are common. Flora like Juniperus, cedar, Ephedra are common to this region.Despite being a cold desert it has patches of grasses and shrubs.

The aquatic ecosystem is both freshwater and marine. Major water bodies are the rivers such as Ganges, Brahmaputra, Godavari and Krishna. Lakes such as Chilika, Dal, Sambhar, Loktak in Manipur and small water bodies like ponds and springs.

The main flora is the water plants, phytoplankton. These rivers are home to fishes, turtles, crocodiles and several aquatic birds.

India has several wetlands like the Wular lake in Jammu and Kashmir and the Vembanad lake in Kerala. These are rich in biodiversity. Both plants and animals are present in these wetlands. Sundarbans has mangrove forests.

Migratory birds like Siberian cranes visit these wetlands. Fauna such as mongoose, mollusks, crustaceans, echinoderms etc. are common.

The marine ecosystem supports diverse marine species like fishes, sharks, marine mammals and seabirds. Coral reefs are present in Andaman and Nicobar Islands, Gulf of Mannar, Lakshadweep islands and Gulf of Kutch. Western Ghats are a UNESCO world heritage site. These are rich in biodiversity. Lion tailed macaque is an endemic species of this biodiversity hotspot.

Ecosystems of Bhutan

Bhutan is a small kingdom in the Eastern Himalayas. The country has a subtropical climate, with heavy rainfall, cool summers and mild winters. It has diverse ecosystems , the dominant being the Forest. Temperate coniferous forests are the most common that consist of the blue pines, chir pine and fir trees. Some broad-leaved trees in both warm and cold climates are present such as Acer, Betula etc.

The evergreen oaks also form a large part of the forest ecosystem. Rhododendrons and Hemlocks also are some of the other flora of the region.

Many species of grasses, herbs and plants of medicinal importance are common in the alpine regions of this country.

Bhutan has a wide variety of plant species. Lichens form an important part of Bhutan biodiversity. The aquatic ecosystem of Bhutan consists of rivers, lakes and a few hot springs and marshes. The main fauna of this ecosystem are the insects, butterflies, reptiles, mammals and bird species. The white bellied Heron, an endangered bird species, is found in Bhutan. Fishes of various types are present in the water bodies of the region.

Ecosystems of Indonesia mainly Bali Region

Bali, an island in Indonesia has green tropical rainforests that are home to many floral species like bamboos, teak and banyan trees. The area supports wildlife like macaques, bird species and nocturnal mammal species civets.

The aquatic ecosystem is formed by rivers such as Ayung, Lakes like Batur that support seagrass and algae. The marine ecosystem of Bali supports marine life like sea turtles, reef sharks and fish species. Coral reefs are also found in some parts of Bali. A mangrove forest is also present near the coastal region. Active volcanoes are common in this region of the globe. Tourism development is a challenge to Bali's ecosystem.

Man made or Artificial Ecosystems

Artificial or man made ecosystems are made by man. They are less diverse and are controlled by humans according to their requirements.These are less stable and the physical factors in such ecosystems are manipulated by humans.Some examples of artificial ecosystems are crop fields, aquariums, spaceships , zoos, botanical gardens etc.

Understanding ecosystems is crucial for addressing environmental challenges of the 21st century. These interconnected systems are important for providing essential services like climate regulation, nutrient cycling and biodiversity support. These support soil conservation, habitat to all organisms and maintain the ecological balance. As anthropogenic pressures intensify, ecosystems are facing threat from climate change, pollution, overexploitation and deforestation.

Conservation and sustainable practices are essential for preserving biodiversity and ensuring a healthy planet for future generations. Thus, protecting and restoring ecosystems is important both socially and morally for a sustainable life on earth.